MACMILLAN CONNECTIONS READING PROGRAM

STEPPING OUT

SENIOR AUTHORS

Virginia A. Arnold   **Carl B. Smith**

AUTHORS

James Flood   **Diane Lapp**

LITERATURE CONSULTANTS

Joan I. Glazer   Margaret H. Lippert

Macmillan/McGraw-Hill School Publishing Company
New York   Chicago   Columbus

ACKNOWLEDGMENTS

The publisher gratefully acknowledges permission to reprint the following copyrighted material:

"Tails" from WHISPERS AND OTHER POEMS by Myra Cohn Livingston. Copyright © 1958 by Myra Cohn Livingston. Reprinted by permission of Marian Reiner for the author.

"Tommy" from BRONZEVILLE BOYS AND GIRLS by Gwendolyn Brooks. Copyright © 1956 by Gwendolyn Brooks Blakely. By permission of Harper & Row, Publishers, Inc.

COVER DESIGN: Josie Yee
FEATURE LOGOS: Eva Burg Vagreti

ILLUSTRATION CREDITS: Terry Burton, 4-9; Yvette Baneck, 16-17; Blanche Sims, 26-33; Linda Solovic, 34-35, 70-71; John Sanford, 36-43; Burt Grodell, 44-45; Patti Boyd, 62-69; John Nez, 72-79.

PHOTO CREDITS: © Robert Lee II, 46-53. © Suzanne Szasz, 11-15, 18-25, 54-61.

Macmillan/McGraw-Hill School Division
866 Third Avenue
New York, New York 10022

Printed in the United States of America

ISBN 0-02-178713-1

9 8 7 6 5 4 3 2 1

Contents

Level 2, STEPPING OUT

The Big Dog

Anne Martin Miranda

Ned sees a big dog.

The big dog likes to jump up.

"You can't jump up on me!" says Ned.

"Get down, big dog.

Get down."

The big dog walks with Ned.

"You can't go in with me!" says Ned.

"Now go, big dog. Go."

The big dog walks in with Ned.

"I can't help it," says Ned.

"The dog likes me.

It likes to jump up on me."

The big dog walks up to the little bag.

Now Ned sees.

The big dog likes the little bag.

"GET DOWN!" says Ned.

"This is my bag.
You can't get it now."

Seeds and the Sun

Virginia A. Arnold

Pat and Jeff like to grow seeds.
"What can the sun do?" says Jeff.

"You can read and see," Pat says.

"The sun can help seeds grow.
You and I can grow seeds," says Jeff.

"I can put in the seeds," says Pat.

"Now I can put the seeds in the sun," Jeff says.

"Water can help seeds grow," says Pat. "I can get the water."

"Jeff, help me with this water," says Pat.
Jeff and Pat put water on the seeds.

"I like to water the seeds with you,"
Jeff says.

"Sun and water help the seeds grow," says Jeff.

"I like to grow seeds," Pat says.

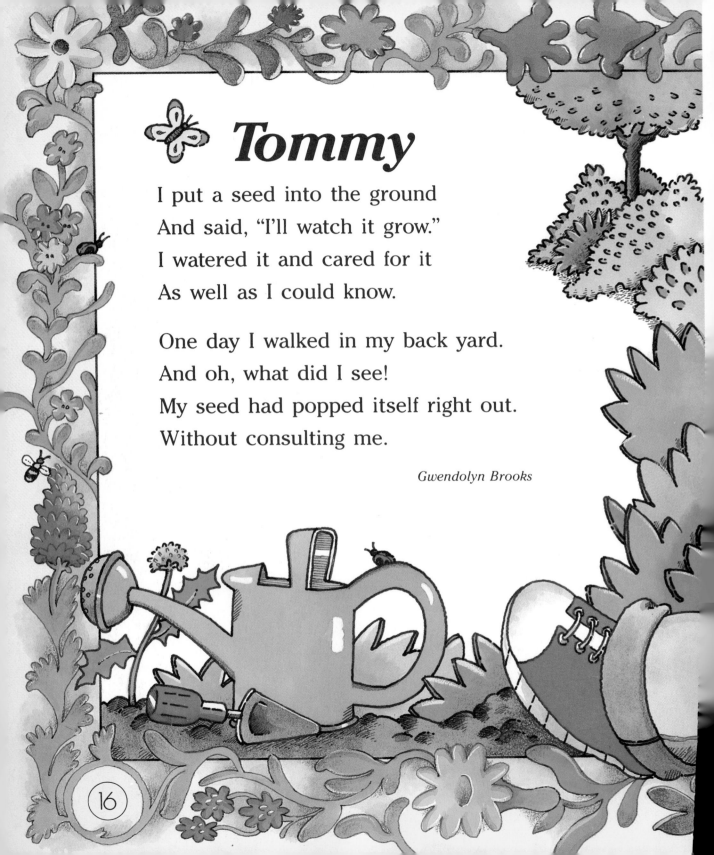

Tommy

I put a seed into the ground
And said, "I'll watch it grow."
I watered it and cared for it
As well as I could know.

One day I walked in my back yard.
And oh, what did I see!
My seed had popped itself right out.
Without consulting me.

Gwendolyn Brooks

The Dog and Pony Show

Gail Schiller Tuchman

Julie Small Gamby

18

Ann and Ted can put on a show.
The show is for boys and girls.

Ann sees a bag.

What can Ann do with it?

"See what I can do," says Ann.

The bag is a dog now.

It is a dog for the show.

Ann can put it on.

Ted sees a bag.

What can Ted do with this bag?

"See what I can do," says Ted.

The bag is a pony now.

It is a pony for the show.

Ted can put it on.

Ann and Ted put on the show.

The boys and girls see the show.

The boys and girls like the show.

What Time Is It?

Anne Martin Miranda

"What time is it?

Can you help me read the clock?"

says Jane.

Tami says, "I can help you.
Look at the big hand.
Look at the little hand.
The big hand and the little hand
show what time it is."

"This is a big help to me," says Jane.

"Jane, what time is it?" says Tami.

"Look at the little hand on the clock."

"It is time for the show," says Jane.

30

Tami says, "Look at the pony.
I can ride on the pony."

Jane says, "Look at the clock!
It is time to go!
Jump down, Tami!"

 Look! Do you see what I see?

 I can get it!

 Come and play, big cat.

 Come and ride, little bird.

 Come with me.
Come and play at night!

 Look at the water.

 Did you see the big fish swim?

Did you see the little fish swim?

40

I can swim!

Jump in!
Jump in the water and swim.

 I like to swim at the zoo.

 Did you see the big cat?

 Help! Help!   I can't swim.

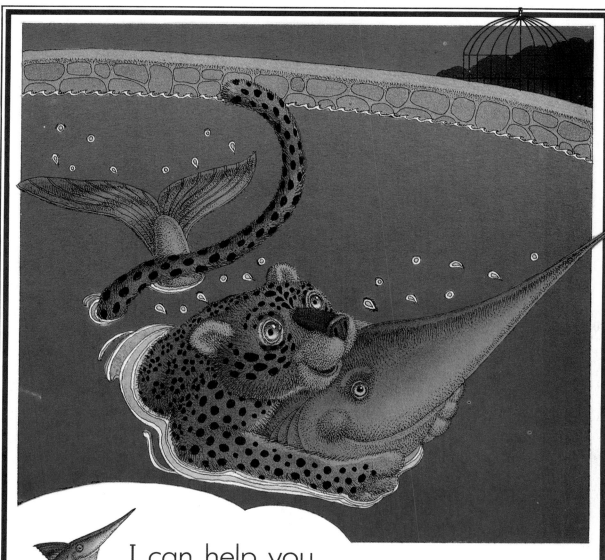

 I can help you.

Now you can ride in the water.

I like to ride in the water.

I like the zoo at night.

TAILS

A dog's tail
is short
And a cat's tail
is long,
And a horse has a tail
that he
swishes along,
And a fish has a tail
that can
help him
to swim,
And a pig has a tail
that looks
curly on him.

44

All monkeys have tails
And the elephants too.
There are
hundreds of
tails
if
you
look
in
the
zoo!

Myra Cohn Livingston

45

MAY I?

Anne Martin Miranda

"It is time to play!" says Jim.

"I like to play *MAY I?*"
says Scott.

"Come on!" says Mary.
Jim, Scott, and Mary go to play.

"May I play with you?" says Jill.

"You may play," Mary says.

"Jim, you go now," says Mary.
"Take a big step."

"May I?" says Jim.

"You may," says Mary.
Jim did take a big step.

"Scott, you take a big step," says Mary.

"May I?" Scott says.

"You may not," says Mary.
"You may not take a big step."
Scott did not take a big step.

"You may take a little step," Mary says.

"May I?" says Scott.

"You may," Mary says.
Scott did take a little step.

Mary says, "Jill, take a big step."

"May I?" says Jill.

"You may," says Mary.
Jill did take a big step.

"Look at Jill!" says Scott.
"Jill is up to Jim."

"I did it!" says Jill.
"I can take a big step like Jim.
I like to play *MAY I?* with you."

COME AND READ

Margaret H. Lippert

Carlos likes to read books on cats.

"Come on!" says Daddy.

"I can help you pick out books."

"Look at the books!" says Carlos. "Daddy, help me pick out a book on cats."

Daddy sees a book on cats.

Carlos sees a big book on the zoo.

"Come and sit down," says Carlos.

Carlos and Daddy sit and read.

Carlos likes to read to Daddy.

Daddy likes to sit and read with Carlos.

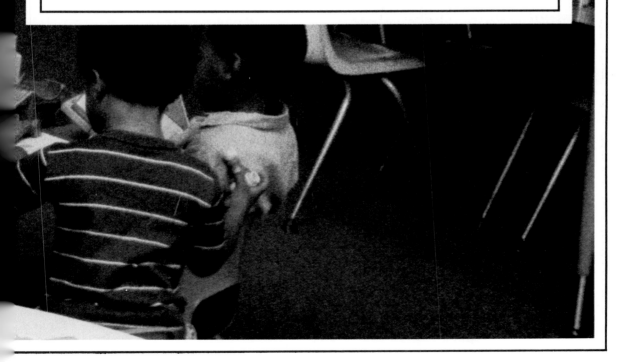

"It is time to go!" says Daddy.
"This is my book.
Did you pick out a book?"

"This is my book!"
says Carlos.
"I like my book."

PAM and the BIG BIRD

Anne Martin Miranda

Pam likes to read at night.

"I like the big bird in this book," she says.

"I wish this bird could come out and play."

She sees the clock.

"It is time to put my book down," she says.

"Wish what you like. Wish what you may.
Now is the time to come and play,"
says the big bird.

"Is it you?" says Pam.
"You look like the bird in my book!"

"Quickly, quickly, come with me.
Wish, Pam! Wish, and you can see,"
says the big bird.

"I wish I could go to the zoo," says Pam.

"I like the zoo!
I like the zoo!
Look, Pam, see what I can do!"
says the big bird.

"Quickly, look at me!" says Pam.

"Look at me!"

The big bird did look up.

"Now I can take a ride!" Pam says.

"I like to come to the zoo at night."

"Is it time to go?" says Pam.

"See the sun. See it grow.
It is time for me to go!"
says the big bird.

"I wish I could go with you," says Pam.

The big bird says,
"You can't go. You can look.
You can see me in the book."

SKILLS activity

Final Consonants

Hear	Read	Write
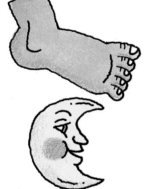	bag hand	<u>bag</u>

 bird   sit   1. _____

 sun   dog   2. _____

 did   big   3. _____

get   look   4. _____

Read	Write
[n] [k̲] Loo__ at the cat.	Look at the cat.

[d] [g] 1. The cat sees the bi__ clock.

[n] [t] 2. The cat ca__ jump up.

[ck] [n] 3. The cat is on the clo__.

[g] [t] 4. The cat can't ge__ down.

[t] [d] 5. Can the cat rea__ the time?

Picture Dictionary

A a

at

Meg and Ned look <u>at</u> the big bird.

B b

book

Mother can help Mark read the <u>book</u>.

books

Mary can help Pat with the <u>books</u>.

boys

The <u>boys</u> play with the dog.

C c

cats

<u>Cats</u> like to sit in the sun.

clock

Look at the <u>clock</u> to see what time it is.

come

"<u>Come</u> with me to the zoo," says Mark.

could

I wish you <u>could</u> come with me.

D d

did

The seeds <u>did</u> grow!

D d

down

You see the sun go <u>down</u> at night.

F f

for

The fish is <u>for</u> the cat.

G g

get

Ned and Pam <u>get</u> books to read.

girls

The <u>girls</u> ride to the park.

grow

What can <u>grow</u> in a park?

H h
hand

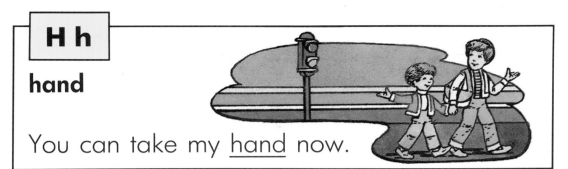

You can take my <u>hand</u> now.

L l
look

Jim and Pam <u>look</u> at books.

M m
may

<u>May</u> I go out to play with Carlos?

N n
night

You can't see the sun at <u>night</u>.

N n

not

"I do <u>not</u> like this," says Ned.

O o

out

Jill walks <u>out</u> of the zoo.

P p

pick

The bird can <u>pick</u> up the seeds.

play

The girls <u>play</u> in the park.

put

Ted <u>put</u> the book in a bag.

Q q

quickly

The man can ride <u>quickly</u> out of the park.

S s

says

Jill <u>says</u>, "I can't play with you now."

seeds

I help my father water the <u>seeds</u>.

she

Meg says <u>she</u> will put the cat out.

show

Pat and Ben take a dog to the pet <u>show</u>.

S s

sit

Scott and Jane <u>sit</u> on the step.

step

Anna can take a little <u>step</u>.

sun

Can you see the <u>sun</u>?

T t

take

"<u>Take</u> my hand," says Mother.

time

It is <u>time</u> for the show.

78

U u

up

Mother says, "Sit <u>up</u>, Jeff."

W w

water

Fish swim in the <u>water</u>.

wish

Nan and Ted <u>wish</u> for a pet.

Z z

zoo

You can see this big cat at the <u>zoo</u>.

Word List

To the teacher: The following words are introduced in *Stepping Out*. The page number to the left of a word indicates where the word first appears in the selection.

   Instructional-Vocabulary words are printed in black. Words printed in red are Applied Skills words that children should be able to decode independently, using previously taught phonics skills.

The Big Dog
5. get
   up
   down
   says

Seeds and the Sun
10. seeds
    sun
    grow
12. put
13. water

The Dog and Pony Show
18. show
19. boys
    girls
    for

What Time Is It?
26. time
28. clock
29. at
    look
    hand

The Zoo at Night
36. zoo
    night
    play
38. come
40. did

May I?
46. may
49. step
    take
50. not

Come and Read
56. pick
    out
    books
    cats
57. book
59. sit

Pam and the Big Bird
63. could
    wish
    she
65. quickly